Mel Bay's First Lessons Harmonica

by David Barrett

Jam Tracks from *C Harmonica Blues Play-Along Tracks* (MB20004CDB)
John Garcia, Guitar; Steve Lucky, Piano; Randy Bermudez, Bass;
Paul Revelli, Drums

Keyboard on Folk Songs Steve Czarnecki

Thanks to Dennis Carelli, Steven Howard, Jon Harl and John Nugent for editing and proof reading.
Thanks to my wife Nozomi, our son Ray and our family both in the US and Japan for their never-ending support.

CD Contents

1 Welcome, A Word from the Author & Material Needed [2:33]
2 Rhythm Training (Ex. 12) [2:28]
3 Getting Started (Ex. 14-15) [0:43]
4 Lovely May (Ex. 16) [1:01]
5 Twinkle, Twinkle Little Star (Ex. 17) [0:34]
6 This Old Man (Ex. 18) [0:26]
7 She'll Be Comin' Around the Mountain (Ex. 19) [0:27]
8 Happy Song (Ex. 20) [0:23]
9 Home Sweet Home (Ex. 21) [0:27]
10 Red River Valley (Ex. 22) [0:27]
11 Row, Row, Row Your Boat (Ex. 23) [0:17]
12 Oh, Susanna! (Ex. 24) [0:30]
13 Jingle Bells (Ex. 25) [0:27]
14 Ex. 28 [0:34]
15 Ex. 29 [0:33]
16 Ex. 30 [0:33]
17 Ex. 31 [0:33]
18 Ex. 32 [0:33]
19 Ex. 33 [0:33]
20 Chugging (Ex. 34-37) [0:43]
21 Throat Vibrato [0:26]
22 Bending (Ex. 38-39) [0:43]
23 Bending (Ex. 40-42) [1:01]
24 The Dip Bend [0:10]
25 Blues Song #1 with Bending (Ex. 43) [0:42]
26 Blues Song #2 with Bending (Ex. 44) [0:42]
27 When the Saints Go Marching In with Bending (Ex. 45) [0:29]
28 Chromatic Scale (Ex. 46) [0:42]
29 Third Position (Ex. 47) [0:15]
30 Third Position Bounce #1 (Ex. 48) [2:40]
31 Tongue Blocking (Ex. 49-51) [0:45]
32 Slap Tongue Blocking (Ex. 52-53) [0:42]
33 Octave Tongue Blocking (Ex. 54-58) [0:52]
34 Ex. 59 [0:43]
35 Ex. 60 [0:42]
36 Third Position Bounce #2 (Ex. 61) [2:40]
37 Third Position Bounce #2 (Ex. 61) Jam Track [2:36]
38 Closing [3:02]

It doesn't get any easier.....

MUSICAL EMPORIUM
L. CASTELLÓ LLOBE... Cia., S.C.
La Rambla 129 – Tel. 317 63 38
08002 BARCELONA

1 2 3 4 5 6 7 8 9 0

Visit us on the Web at www.melbay.com — E-mail us at email@melbay.com

Table of Contents

 Tr. 1

A Word from the Author

Welcome to Mel Bay's *First Lessons Harmonica*. My name is David Barrett, and I'm the author of this book and the *Harmonica Masterclass Complete Blues Harmonica Lesson Series* by Mel Bay Publications. Harmonica is a wonderful instrument that offers people of all ages the chance to express themselves through music. To play an instrument well takes hard work and perseverance. With good study habits and a genuine desire to learn how to play, you will do just fine.

After you have completed this book, refer to the back cover for details about more advanced harmonica instruction books available. You should expect this material to take you from two to six months study time to complete if you have an hour practice time each day. Don't worry if you're on the longer end of this time line. Some people excel with beginning material, others struggle in the beginning and really shine with the later, more advanced studies. Work with this material at your own pace. Enjoy your practice time, don't be in a hurry. To play an instrument well is a lifetime pleasure.

If you have any questions regarding this book, or any other books I have authored, look at the Harmonica Masterclass website at www.harmonicamasterclass.com, or contact me by mail at PO Box 1723, Morgan Hill, CA 95038. Good luck and have fun!

Material Needed

Harmonica You will need a C major ten-hole diatonic harmonica for this book and recording.

CD Player Whether you are studying this course by yourself or with a harmonica instructor, the CD included with this book will be very helpful to make sure your notes are correct and your rhythm is strong.

Understanding Notated Music

Staff: The music staff has five lines. Time moves from left to right on the staff.

Ex. 1

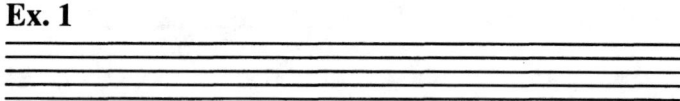

Ledger Lines: The lower lines hold notes that are low in pitch. The upper lines hold notes that are high in pitch. Sometimes notes go beyond the five lines and ledger lines are used to help keep your place.

Ex. 2

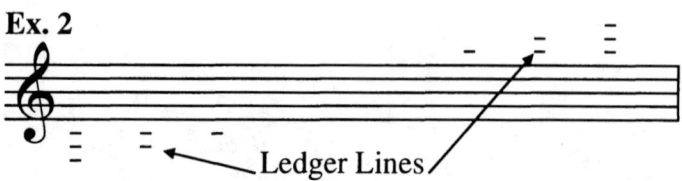

Treble Clef: The treble clef symbol is placed at the beginning of a staff to give a reference pitch. You can see that the bottom curl encircles the second line from the bottom. This second line is the pitch G. Because of this, the treble clef is also known as the *G Clef.*

Ex. 3

Notes on the Lines: Notes are found on each line of the staff and ledger lines. The notes **E G B D F** found on the staff can be remembered by using "Every Good Boy Does Fine."

Ex. 4

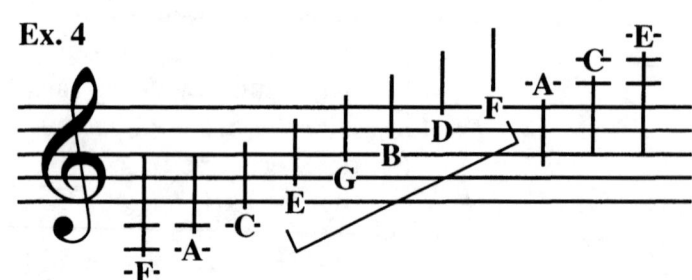

Notes in the Spaces: Notes are also found in the spaces. The notes *F A C E* found on the staff can be remembered by using **"FACE."**

Ex. 5

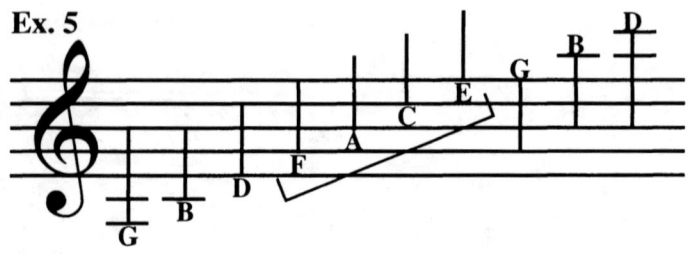

Stem Direction: Notes are placed on these lines and spaces that tell you how long to hold a note. You will see notes that have stems. Some stems point upward and some stems point downward. Stem direction does not change the pitch or length of a note.

Ex. 6

Time Signature, Bar Line & Ending: The line that dissects the staff is called a ***Bar Line.*** The time between two bar lines is called a ***Measure.*** The thin bar line and thick bar line at the end of the staff tells you that the song is over. The ***Time Signature*** is placed at the beginning of a piece of music to tell you how many beats are in a measure and which note duration is to receive the beat. The 4/4 time signature shows that there are four beats per measure and the quarter note receives the beat.

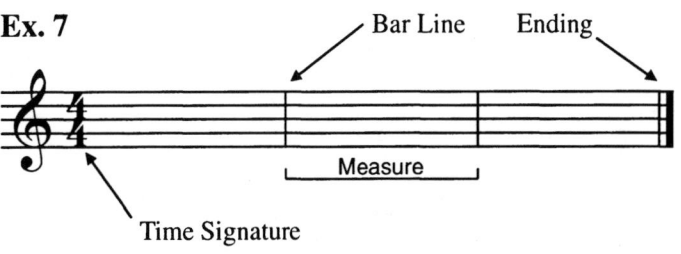

Note Durations: A whole note is held for a count of four beats, or one whole measure. A half note is held for a count of two beats, or half a measure. A quarter note is held for one beat, or one quarter of a measure.

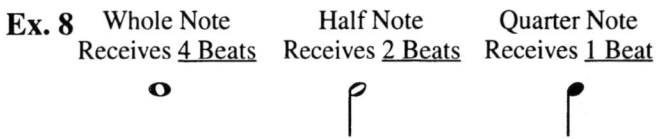

Pitch & Duration on the Staff: This example shows: the 4/4 time signature; a C whole note for the first measure; a C half note and A half note for the second measure; and B, A, G, and F quarter notes for the third measure.

The example below demonstrates the common rhythms we'll use that subdivide the beat. The example starts with quarter notes to show that each quarter note lands on the beat. To the right of the quarter note is the eighth note, which has two notes per beat (each worth a half beat). The Sixteenth rhythm is four notes to the beat (each worth one quarter of a beat). The triplet rhythm is three notes to the beat (each worth a third of a beat). This is shown below in example 10.

When a dot is added to a note, it extends its value by half. A half note with a dot equals three beats and a quarter note with a dot equals a beat and a half. All notes also have a corresponding rest. When seeing these, you will not play. This is shown below in example 11.

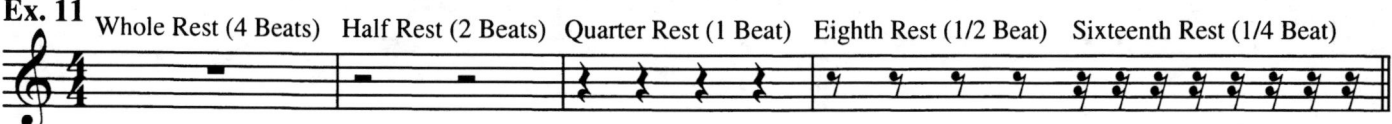

5

Rhythm Training

Due to the harmonica having numbered holes, most players will "play by the numbers" and not go into the reading of music (especially blues, country and rock harmonica players). The information is here, so take advantage of it if you wish to learn how to read. I think it's a great idea. Whether you stay with the harmonica or move on to another instrument, the skills gained by reading music will stay with you.

Even if you decide to just use the hole numbers and not read the notes, understanding the rhythm notation is very helpful. I spend a little bit of time doing rhythm training with all my private students, even my students that are professional players. Detailed below is an example that will help you to become familiar with the rhythms we just defined in the previous pages.

Tr. 2

Ex. 12

Called a "Tie" and combines the duration of two notes.

Placing Your Lips on the Harmonica

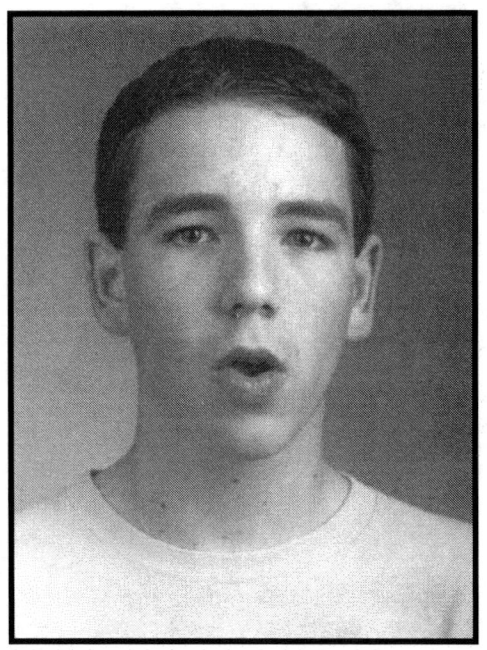

The *Tilted Embouchure* is achieved by opening your mouth as pictured left. Place the harmonica in your mouth with the front of the harmonica tilted downward as pictured right. With slight pressure, press the harmonica into your bottom lip. If you hear a little bit of either adjacent hole, tilt the harmonica more, or bring the sides of your lips in a bit. The jaw should be low, the tongue should sit on the floor of the mouth and the throat should be open. Yawning will help to give you

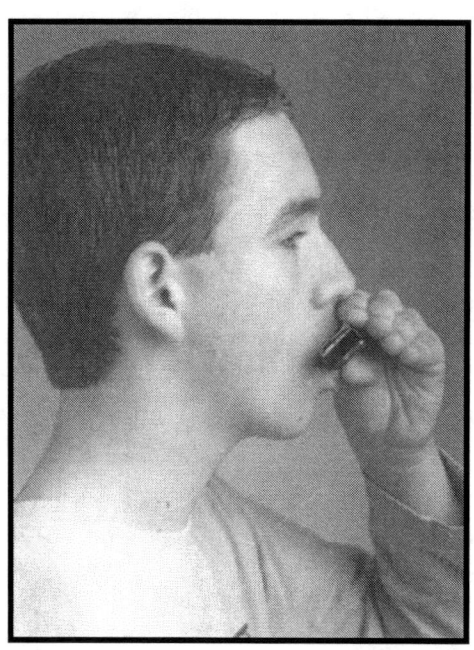

the sensation of this embouchure. This will create an unrestricted passage for your air to travel. If the tongue raises, it most likely will cause your notes to sound flat, airy, or not sound at all.

Holding the Harmonica

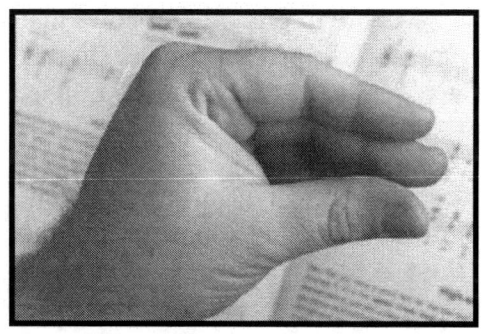

The first rule of holding the harmonica is to not cover your playing surface. Notice in the pictures above that the upper lip covers a large area of the top cover plate. Make sure that your fingers do not get in the way of your lip placement.

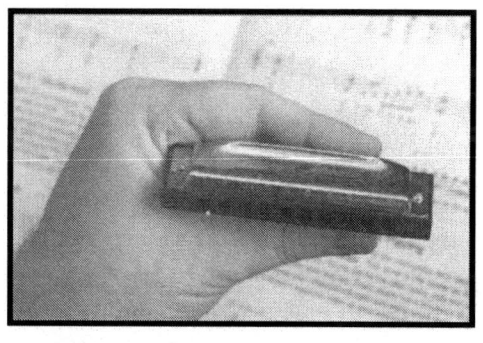

Pictured (above) left is how your left hand should look before placing the harmonica in your hand. Pictured (above) right shows how the harmonica sits in that cradle. The harmonica might fall out at this point. Therefore, we need the other hand and your lips to help seat the harmonica. Pictured below and to the left shows where your right hand is placed.

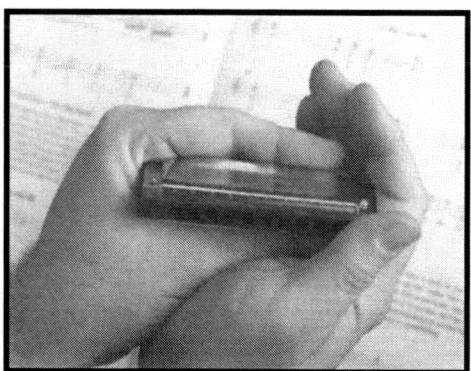

Do not close the back of your cupped hands; we want the sound to go to the listener. Pictured at right is how the back of your hands are open and relaxed. If you want to practice quietly, you can close the back of your hands to cup in the sound. The tighter you cup, the less sound that comes out.

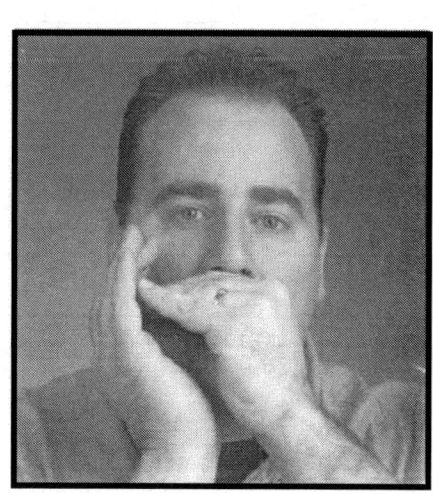

Getting Started

The holes of your harmonica are numbered from one to ten. Hole number one (left end) is the lowest note on the harmonica with the notes getting higher as you slide to the right to number ten. The harmonica can be both blown upon and drawn upon to create a note. Hole numbers are present below the music notation to tell where that pitch is found on the harmonica. When the hole number is followed by a plus you are to blow (4+ = four blow). When a note stands by itself you are to draw (inhale). For this book we will be using the C major diatonic harmonica. Your first step in learning the harmonica is to memorize the notes available; this is diagramed below.

Ex. 13

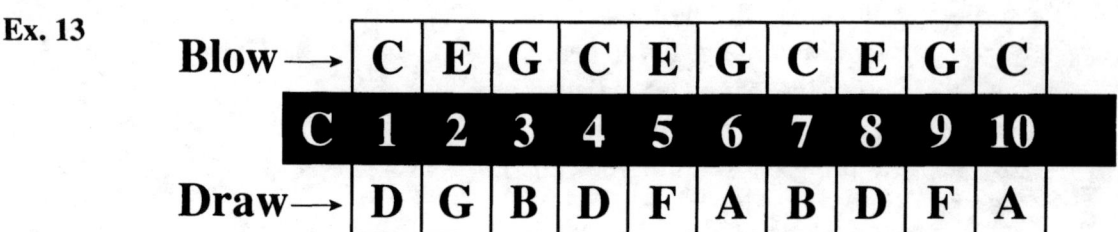

Let's start by learning the essential notes of our harmonica. Placed in ascending and descending order, these notes construct the **C Major Scale.** The C major scale is complete from the 4 blow to the 7 blow. This is the range we will use most on the harmonica when playing folk tunes. From the 7 to 10 blow there is one note of scale missing, B. This note can be produced through bending (a technique we will learn later), but the note is not commonly used—so no worries. The 1 to 4 blow has two missing notes, again obtainable through bending as we study that later.

The question this brings up is "why are there missing notes?" The harmonica is built with two concepts in mind. One, the major scale (the notes from which melodies are made) is available with a combination of blows and draws. Two, when placing your lips over more than one hole, you produce a chord (a grouping of notes that sound good when played together). Due to the mixture of these two, sometimes one impedes the other. In this case, the note selection to produce the desired chord on the bottom range of the harmonica (1-4) was more important than having all of the notes of the scale.

Your main focus here is to achieve good single notes (no bleeding of adjacent holes) with good tone (not flat, airy or thin in tone). If your notes sound flat, or won't sound at all, your tongue is humped up in the back of the mouth. Drop the back of the tongue down to get it out of the way. You may need to open your mouth in front of a mirror to check your tongue's position.

8

Folk Songs

To help you learn to move around the harmonica, it's best to start with songs which you already know the melody and rhythm. In some areas you will see a comma notated above the music. These are areas where it's a good idea to inhale or exhale to balance your breath.

Tr. 4

Ex. 16–Lovely May

Tr. 5

Ex. 17–Twinkle, Twinkle Little Star

Tr. 6

Ex. 18–This Old Man

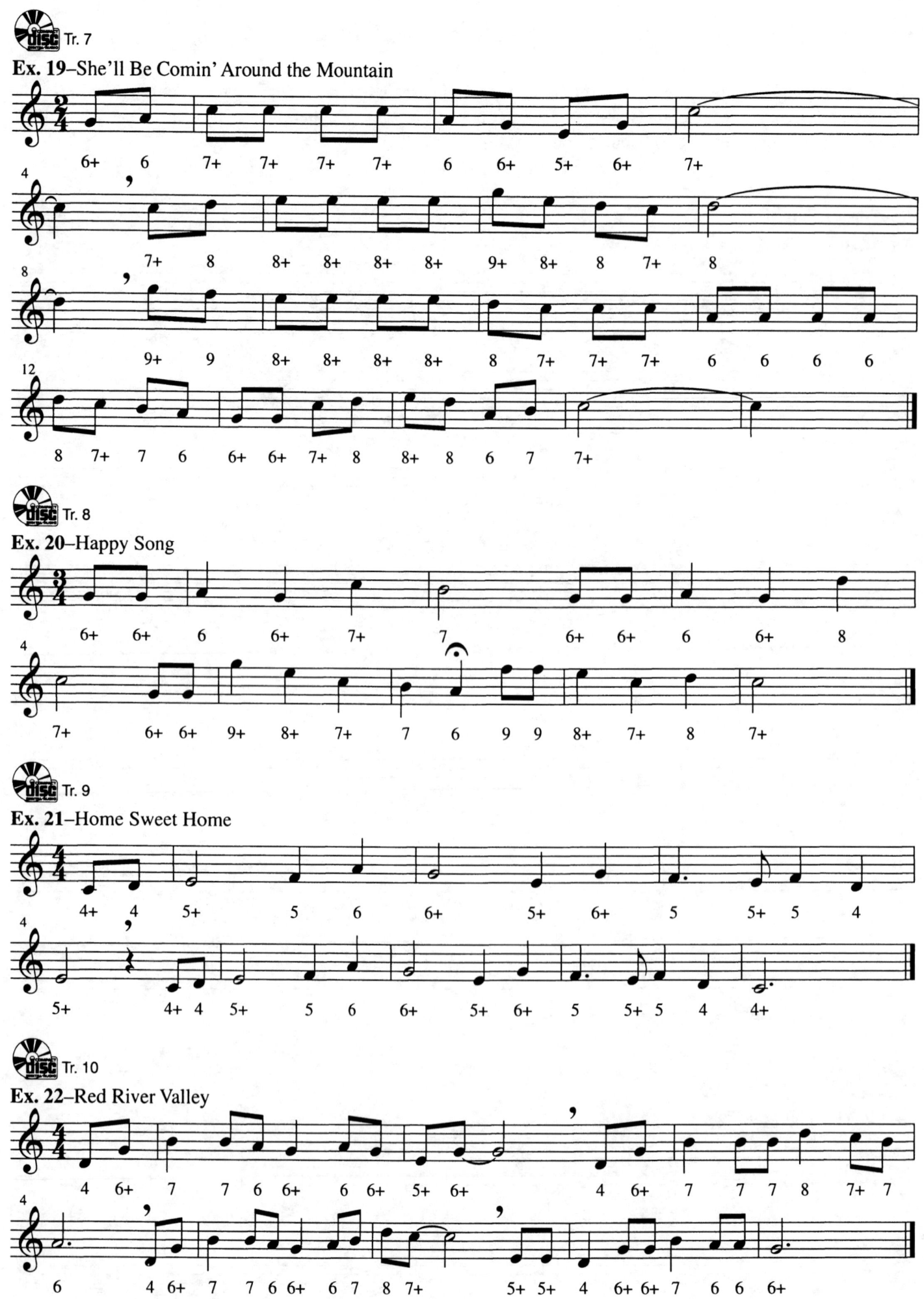

Ex. 23–Row, Row, Row Your Boat

Ex. 24–Oh, Susanna!

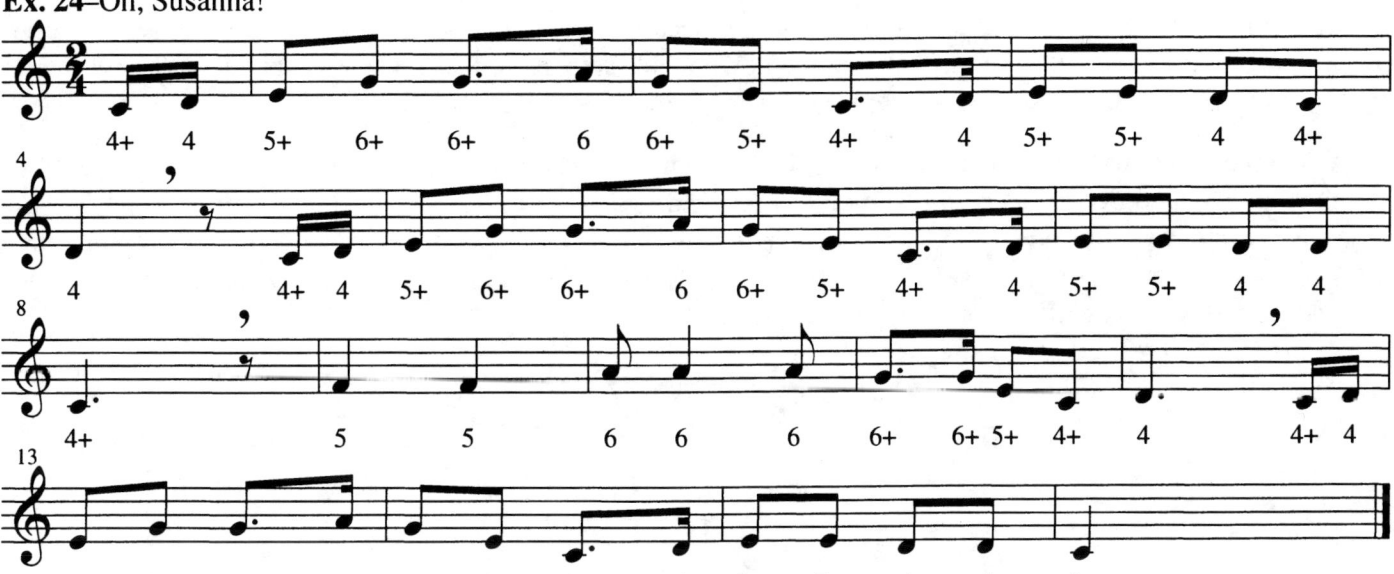

Ex. 25–Jingle Bells

Understanding Blues & Second Position

So far we have been playing a C harmonica in the key of C, using the C major scale. It is also possible to play our C harmonica in other keys. The key of G uses six of the same notes as C (G, A, B, C, D and E), with the seventh note raised (F is played as F#). Because these scales are so similar, it makes playing in G possible. Demonstrated below is the C major scale, with the G major scale next to it for comparison.

Ex. 26

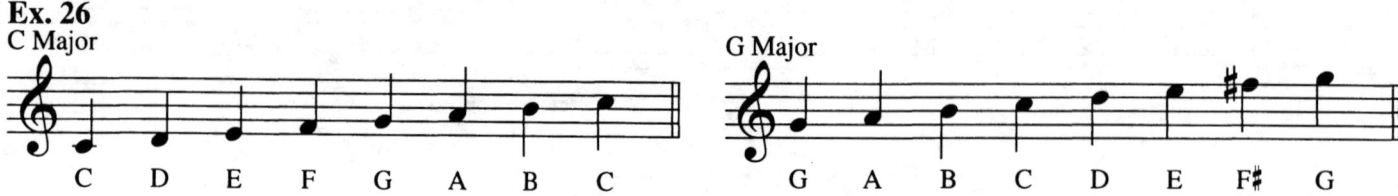

Because we are playing on a C harmonica, which does not have the note F#, the F# is played as F natural. This, in essence, lowers the seventh scale degree down a half step and creates a bluesy sound. In the following blues songs you will notice when the note F is played (5 draw), it will sound bluesy.

When playing your C harmonica in the key of G (five notes up from the key of the harmonica), you are playing in what is called *Second Position,* sometimes referred to as *Cross Harp.* Second position has some advantages over *First Position* (playing a C harmonica in the key of C). When playing in second position, it places our most important notes on the draw side of the harmonica. The draw side is where most of our bends are available. Diagramed below is a bend chart of the harmonica.

Ex. 27

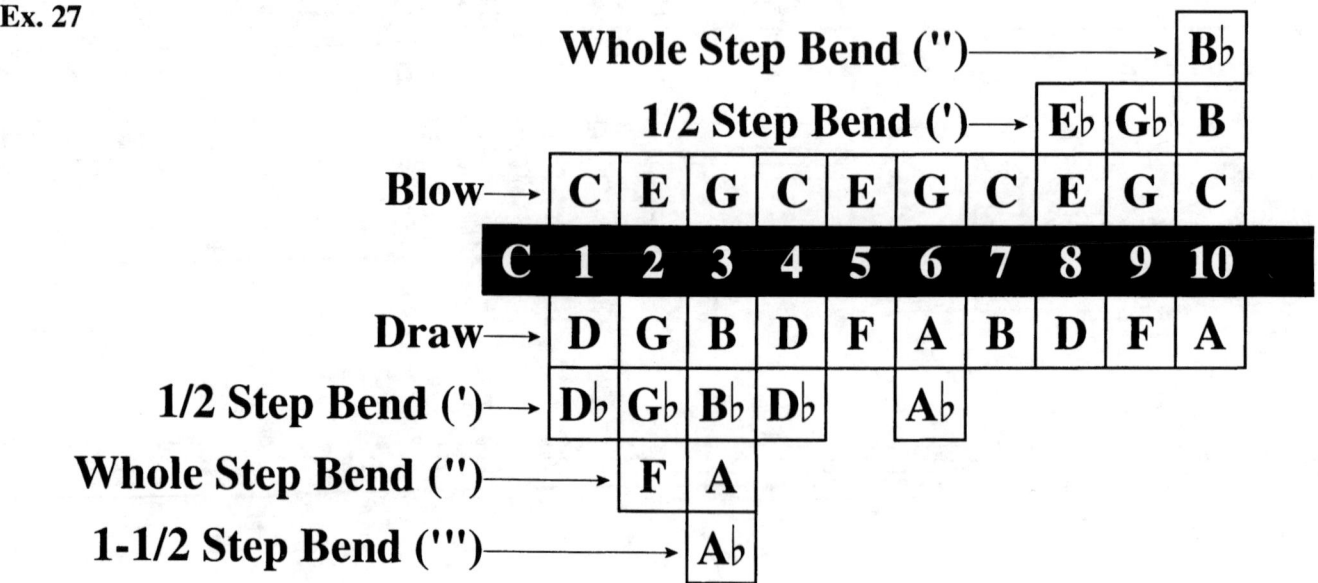

Bending gives us much more expression on the harmonica, allowing us to slide into or out of notes. It also helps us to produce notes that were not previously available in certain ranges. Second position is the preferred position of most blues, country and rock harmonica players.

I understand that this is all pretty abstract at the moment, but as you play and study more, these principles will become more clear over time. Let's play some blues!

Blues Songs

The following blues songs we will play with guitarist John Garcia. The first time through (called one chorus) I will play. When studying the following songs, take each separate piece of the music (called licks) and work on them separately. After each piece feels good, then try stringing them together and playing along with John on the track.

Our first example will start with a simple rhythmic figure to help you get a feel for blues. The songs will get progressively more difficult. Take your time and be patient, some of the songs will take weeks, sometimes months to play well. Also notice that the notation has been moved up an octave on the staff. This makes reading music easier for the lower range blues prefers.

Ex. 33

Chugging

The ten hole major diatonic harmonica is tuned to play single note melodies from the 4th hole and above, and chords from the 4th hole and below. By playing two to four notes at a time you create a chord. The lick examples below use chording and the swing rhythm to create a portion of the blues progression. This type of rhythmic chord playing is called *Chugging*.

When blowing or drawing on the harmonica, keep your nose closed at all times. If your nose is open while playing a long note, or a string of notes using breath in one direction, you will run out of air before you finish. In later books you will learn how to regulate air with your nose for longer passages. For now, none of the passages in this book require any tricky breath patterns where the nose is used.

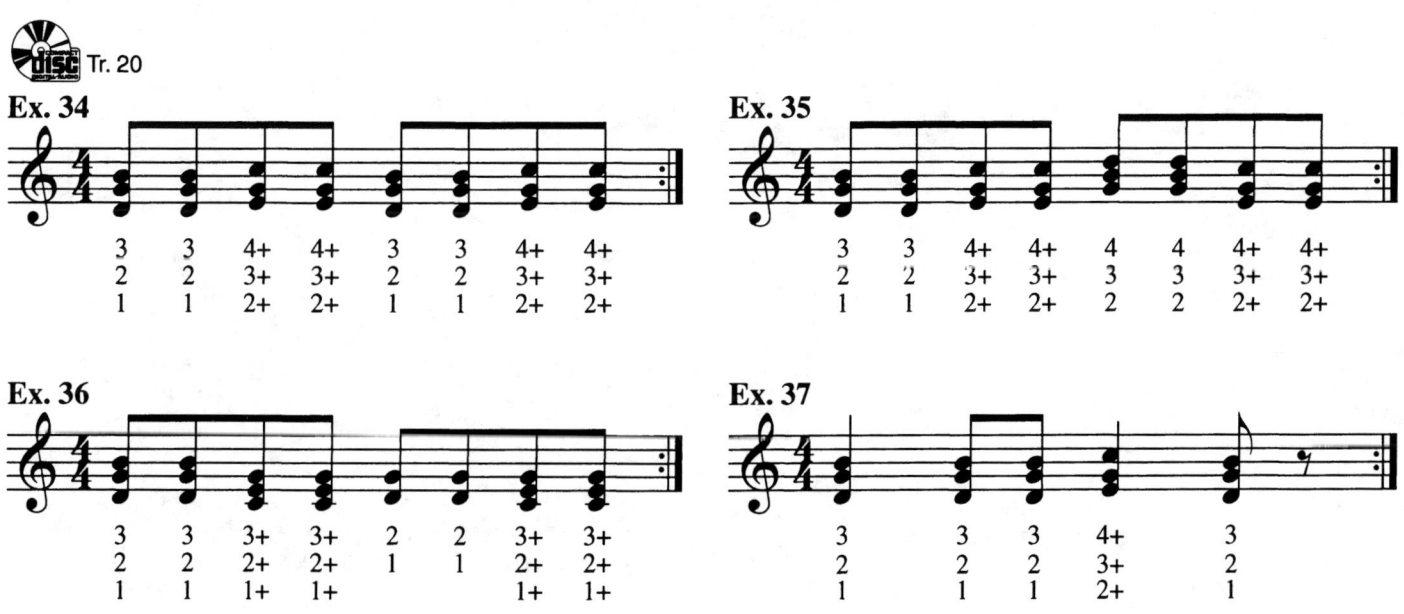

Ex. 34   **Ex. 35**

Ex. 36   **Ex. 37**

New Technique – Throat Vibrato

Whenever you hold a note, you'll want to add a vibrato in most cases. There are four types of Vibrato on the harmonica: hand, laughing (tremolo), staccato (more articulated tremolo), and bent vibrato (a true textbook vibrato). Within this book we'll focus on the most used laughing vibrato. To get a feel for this vibrato start by exhaling and coughing lightly in a rhythmic fashion. When your vocal folds close, no air comes out. When your vocal folds open, air is released. The cough is caused by (1) starting with closed vocal folds, (2) the build-up of pressure behind the vocal folds from the diaphragm, (3) and the release of air, making the cough sound. Our vibrato is produced in the same fashion. As we exhale or inhale air through the harmonica, our vocal folds open and close rhythmically to give a pulsating sound. This quick, rhythmic change of volume gives us the tremolo affect we use for our main vibrato.

Blow vibrato is usually not too hard to produce, but the draw vibrato commonly takes longer for most people to achieve. After all, how many times have you coughed inhaling? Make sure you're not saying Ka Ka Ka with your tongue; it can approximate the same sound, but is not correct.

Take any example that you've played so far that includes notes that are held for more than one beat and play those notes with a vibrato.

David Barrett teaching at his Harmonica Masterclass® Workshops

Bending

Now that you can move around the harmonica with good tone and rhythm, it's time to start learning how to bend. Because the process of bending happens solely in the mouth where you can't see what's happening, we'll need to spend a lot of time describing the process so that you have all the tools you need to figure out this great technique.

How it Works

Bending is achieved by two movements of the tongue. The tongue must move up to constrict the air passage and the tongue must move back to pull the pitch down.

The passageway for a bend is best felt starting with saying the vowel E. E places the middle/back of the tongue under the upper set of teeth. This sets up the passage where the air will travel. You can feel the air only traveling between the roof of your mouth, the inner-sides of your teeth, and the top of your tongue. The center of the tongue then pushes up (the sides of the tongue stay on the teeth in most cases) to squeeze the air stream for the constriction needed. The tongue then pulls back to bring the pitch of that reed down. Depending where you hump up your tongue, you might have very little movement back for the bend (such as a 6 draw), or you might have a large amount of movement to create the bend (such as the 3, 2 and 1 draw).

Each reed is a different length, and different sounding pitch. The longer the reed, the lower the pitch and the slower its vibration. The shorter the reed, the higher its pitch and the faster its vibration. In the bending process, as you move your tongue back for the bend, it's frequency pulling the reed. In other words, as your tongue moves back, the resonant pitch of your mouth lowers. This is best felt by whistling. Try to whistle a high note, then slowly slide the pitch down to the lowest note you can achieve. Do you notice your tongue is touching your upper set of teeth and to lower the pitch you move your tongue back, and to raise the pitch your tongue moves forward. The process is the same for bending a note on the harmonica.

For the 6 draw, your tongue moves up, and not very much back. For the 4 draw, you will move further up and back. You will probably find the 4 draw to be one of your easier notes to bend. When trying the 3 or 2 draw bend, most players don't move their tongue up high enough and far enough back. The 3 draw bend is achieved by having your tongue humped up in the back, pushing behind the back molars, resting on the gums. The 2 draw is further back, most of the time not touching the teeth at all, just the gums. The 1 draw is back and down a bit.

Keep in mind bending is achieved by two movements of the tongue. The tongue must move up to constrict the air passage and the tongue must move back to pull the pitch down. When having difficulties in bending, try moving your tongue more up than back, or more back than up, or more back and up, or less back and up. The main point is to experiment!

What Notes Can Bend

Not every hole (note) on the harmonica can be bent, and not every hole that you can bend allows the same degree of bend. The amount of bend you can achieve is dictated by the distance (interval) between your draw and blow reed.

Notated below is the chromatic scale. The chromatic scale lists every note available in music.

 Tr. 22

Ex. 38

A B♭ B C D♭ D E♭ E F G♭ G A♭ A

Let's look at the 1 draw and the 1 blow. The 1 draw is the note D and the 1 blow is the note C. When playing a 1 draw bend, you can bend down to whatever note is between these two notes. Looking at the chromatic scale above, that gives you the note D flat. When playing a 2 draw bend, you can bend down to whatever is between the G of the 2 draw and E of the 2 blow. This gives you the notes G flat and F. Follow this rule up to the 6 draw.

At the seventh hole the harmonica does a back flip of sorts. On holes 1 through 6, the draw notes are higher than the blow notes (1 draw D is higher in the scale than 1 blow C for example). On the seventh through tenth holes the blows are now higher than the draws. This means that you will bend the blow notes now. The same rule applies for the blow notes… whatever pitches are between the blow and draw reed is what you can bend.

Diagramed below are all the bends available on the C harmonica. Each slash represents a half step bend (3 = 3 draw, 3' = 3 draw half step bend, 3" = 3 draw whole step bend and 3'" = 3 draw minor third bend).

Ex. 39

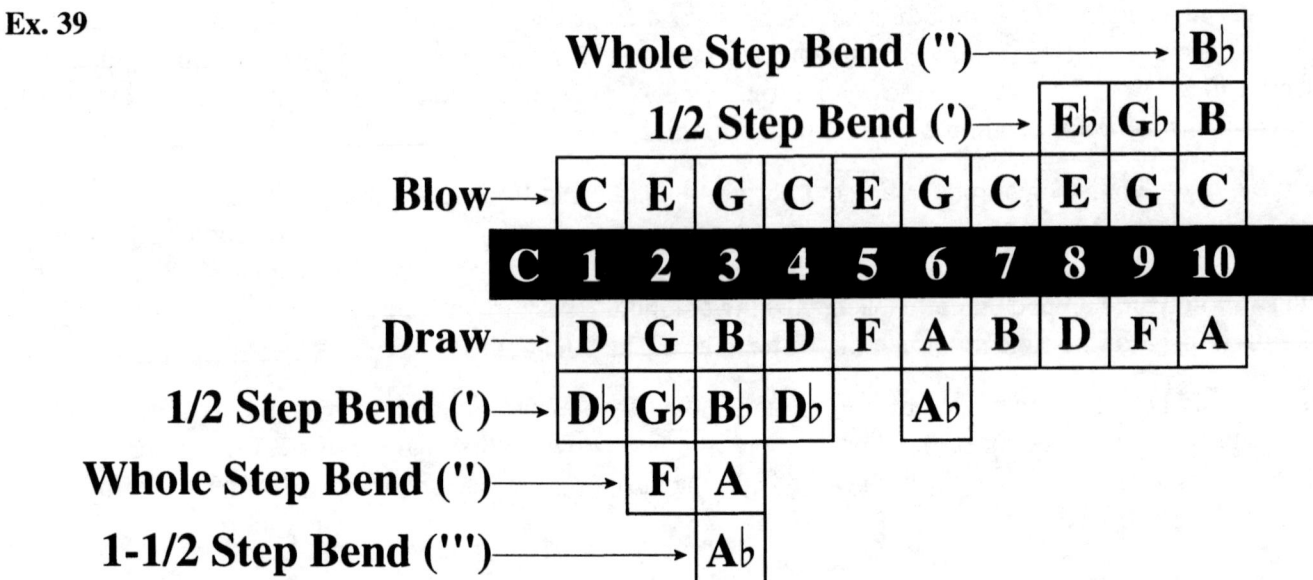

Bending Exercises

Your first goal is to bend as far as you can on each of the holes in the next exercises. Most people find the 6, 5 and 4 draw the easiest holes to bend. Take note that the 5 draw will not give you a full degree of a bend, it will bend down what is called a **Quartertone.** In other words, you will only hear a slight bend on the 5 draw and that is correct. The 3 and 2 draw will be very challenging. Expect these two holes to take months before they start to bend consistently.

Ex. 40

The exercises below will help you to bend a note down and move to another note. Pay attention that your bend doesn't release slightly before going to the next note. Also pay attention that your next note is not played flat because you haven't moved your tongue out of the bend embouchure quick enough.

Ex. 41

Ex. 42

New Technique – Dip Bend

The *Dip Bend* is a bend, but is more in the category of an articulation. The dip bend starts a note with a slight lowering in pitch and immediately comes back to pitch. The dip bend can be articulated using TYA or KYA. Listen to and practice with the recording for this new technique. The dip bend can be used on any bendable note when you want to add a little flavor to the start of a note. The dip bend is notated by a "v" above the note head of the note that you are to use the dip bend.

Songs That Use Bending

Blues #1

This song will help you work on bending a note to the bottom for expression.

Ex. 43

Blues #2

This song works on bending a note down and going to the next note unbent. Take your time, this song will be one of the most challenging yet.

Folk Song

Some songs require bends to be played as true to pitch as possible. As you try "When the Saints Go Marching In" (Ex. 45), you will hear that the 3 draw bend (3") needs to be dead on pitch to sound good. At this stage of your playing and bending skills this will be very challenging. As your skills progress, bends will be thought of as notes that can be used any time, in any combination. The development of bending skills are pretty high on the list of what things harmonica players must perform confidently before they can really start to play good pieces.

 Tr. 27

Ex. 45

Chromatic Scale

We saw the chromatic scale when we looked at what notes where available on the harmonica for bending. The chromatic scale is every note possible in music in ascending and descending order on our instrument. Using the chromatic scale, let's identify what notes can and can't be created with both natural (unbent) and bent notes. As you will see, there are some notes not available, but all in all, there are a lot of notes available on the harmonica with the addition of bending. This is more for information right now; to bend these notes and hold them to pitch is a little over and above our studies at the moment, but it's good to look at what you're shooting for in the long run.

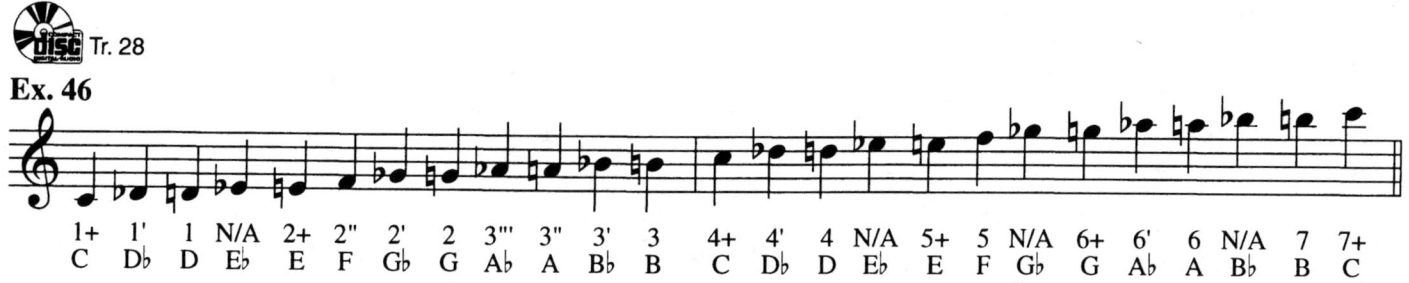

Tr. 28

Ex. 46

1+	1'	1	N/A	2+	2"	2'	2	3'''	3"	3'	3	4+	4'	4	N/A	5+	5	N/A	6+	6'	6	N/A	7	7+
C	Db	D	Eb	E	F	Gb	G	Ab	A	Bb	B	C	Db	D	Eb	E	F	Gb	G	Ab	A	Bb	B	C

Third Position

The following two pages contain your first full-length blues song. It is written in what is called *Third Position*. To play in third position, you play your C harmonica in the key of D (one step higher than the key of the harmonica). This places your home base on D (1, 4 and 8 draw). The D scale, as available on your C harmonica without bending, is notated below.

Tr. 29

Ex. 47

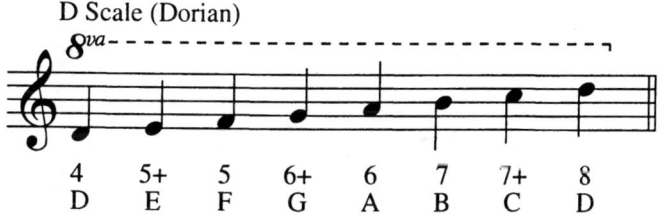

D Scale (Dorian)

4	5+	5	6+	6	7	7+	8
D	E	F	G	A	B	C	D

Take your time on the following song. The speed at which some of the bending is used will be very challenging at first. Play the song slowly at first, gradually building speed as your skills develop and you become more familiar with the song.

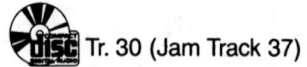

Ex. 48–Third Position Bounce

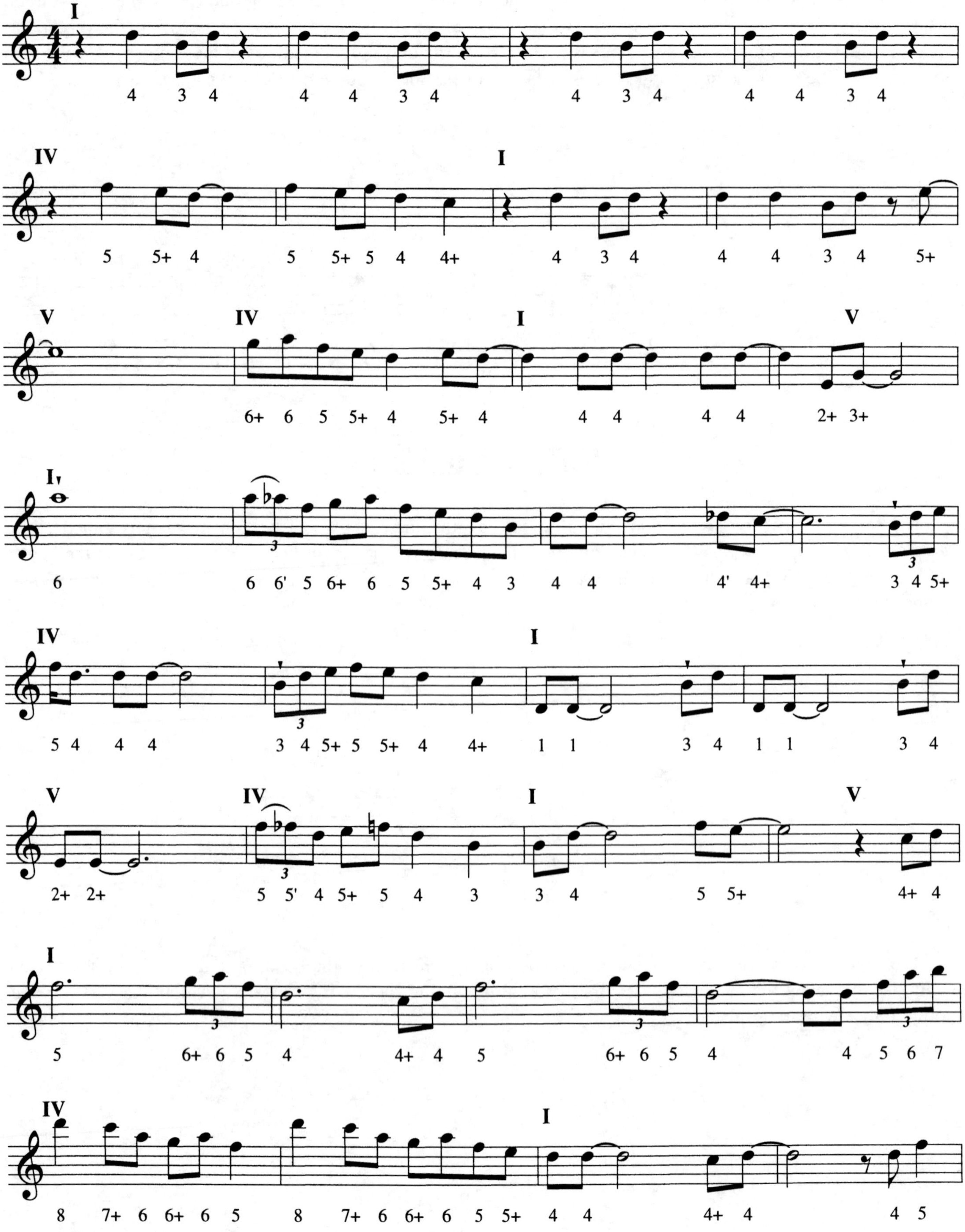

I

4 3 4   4 4 3 4   4 3 4   4 4 3 4

IV   I

5 5+ 4   5 5+ 5 4 4+   4 3 4   4 4 3 4 5+

V   IV   I   V

6+ 6 5 5+ 4 5+ 4   4 4   4 4   2+ 3+

I♭

6   6 6' 5 6+ 6 5 5+ 4 3 4 4   4' 4+   3 4 5+

IV   I

5 4 4 4   3 4 5+ 5 5+ 4 4+   1 1   3 4 1 1   3 4

V   IV   I   V

2+ 2+   5 5' 4 5+ 5 4 3   3 4   5 5+   4+ 4

I

5   6+ 6 5 4   4+ 4 5   6+ 6 5 4   4 5 6 7

IV   I

8 7+ 6 6+ 6 5   8 7+ 6 6+ 6 5 5+ 4 4   4+ 4   4 5

22

23

Tongue Blocking

In previous blues songs you might have noticed a chordal sound before some of the notes. This is achieved through the use of *Tongue Blocking.* Tongue blocking has the same objective as playing with a puckered embouchure… to create a single note. Tongue blocking is achieved by placing your lips over four holes and blocking the three holes to the left with your tongue, leaving the right hole to sound. The diagram below demonstrates this.

Tr. 31

Ex. 49

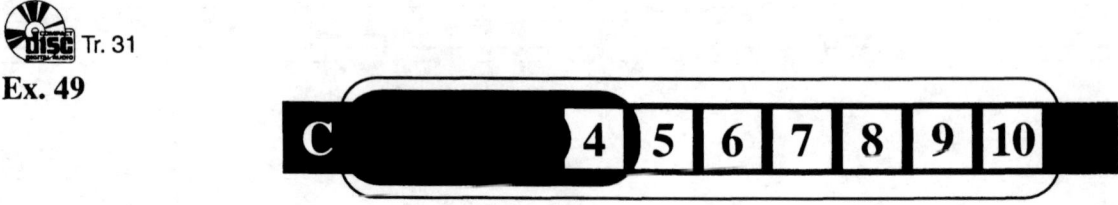

Try playing the C major scale below to practice this new technique.

Ex. 50

C Major

4+ 4 5+ 5 6+ 6 7 7+ 7+ 7 6 6+ 5 5+ 4 4+

Let's play "Oh, Susanna" again with the tongue block embouchure.

Ex. 51–Oh, Susanna! (Tongue Blocked)

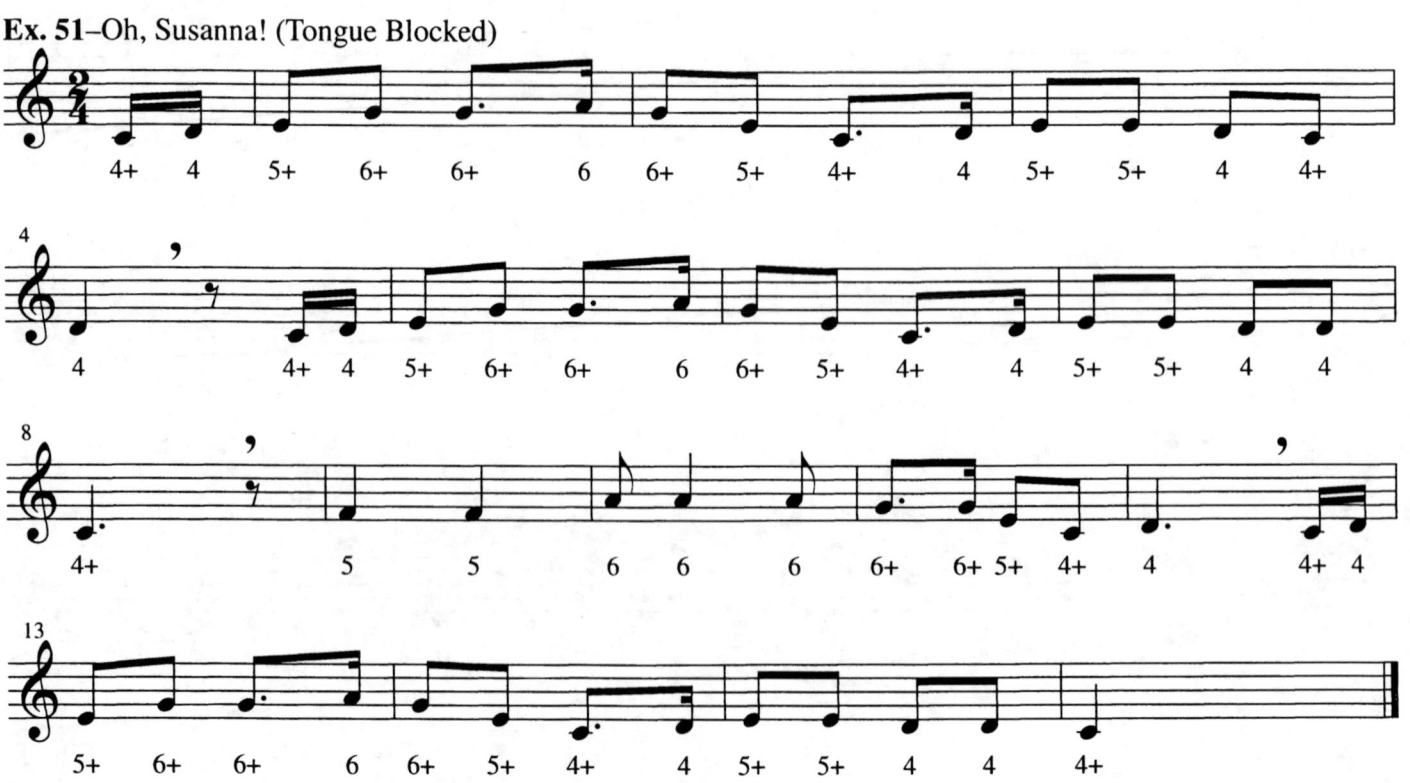

4+ 4 5+ 6+ 6+ 6 6+ 5+ 4+ 4 5+ 5+ 4 4+

4 4+ 4 5+ 6+ 6+ 6 6+ 5+ 4+ 4 5+ 5+ 4 4

4+ 5 5 6 6 6 6+ 6+ 5+ 4+ 4 4+ 4

5+ 6+ 6+ 6 6+ 5+ 4+ 4 5+ 5+ 4 4 4+

24

Tongue Slaps

Did you hear any difference from the first time you played it with a pucker embouchure? I bet you didn't. The tongue block's goal is to just play a single note, just like the pucker. The difference comes in when you use the technique we call the tongue slap. A *Tongue Slap* is achieved by starting with the tongue off the harmonica, breathing, then slapping the tongue down over the three holes to the left, leaving the right hole to sound. This gives you a full chord before each single note. This technique is used often. Written below is the same C major scale exercise and "Oh, Susanna" again, but with the use of the tongue slap. The open circle above each note head designates the use of the slap.

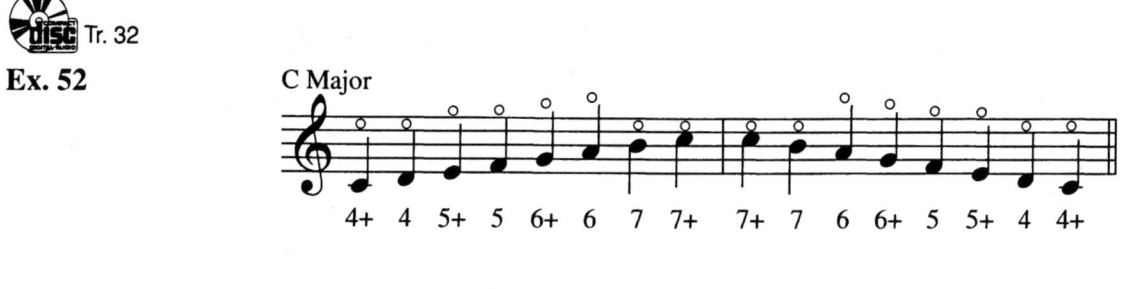

Tr. 32

Ex. 52

Octaves

Did you notice the full sound it gives the song? Tongue slaps are really great. Another great tongue blocking technique is the octave. The *Octave* embouchure is achieved by placing your lips over four holes, blocking the two middle holes, leaving the hole on the left and right to sound. Looking at the C harmonica note chart, notice that you can play octaves (playing two notes of the same name, one octave apart) on all of the blow notes from the 4 blow and above. This is demonstrated on the next page.

Ex. 54

Ex. 55

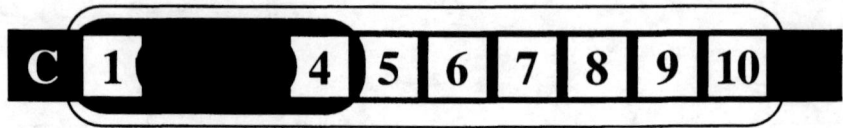

Ex. 56

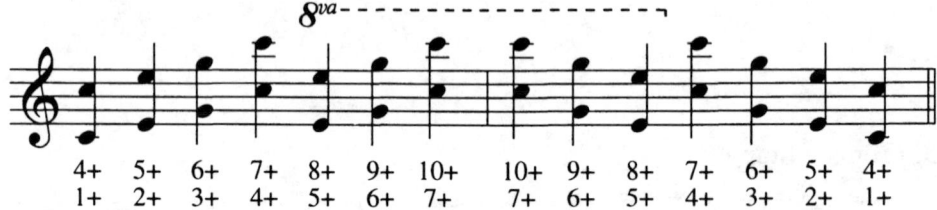

The draw octaves are for the most part dissonant. The 4 draw octave is OK, but as soon as you play the fifth hole, you can see and hear that they are not matching notes. We can still use them, though they can sound a little out of place. This is demonstrated below.

Ex. 57

Once you hit the seventh hole draw, octaves are available if you were to open your lips over five holes, blocking the three holes in the middle with your tongue. This technique is a little too advanced right now, so we'll just focus on the four hole octave embouchure. Let's play "Oh, Susanna" again with octaves. Notice that the draw notes work, though they sound dissonant at times.

Ex. 58–Oh, Susanna! (Octaves)

Ex. 61–Third Position Bounce

About the Author

David Barrett is the world's most published author of blues harmonica lesson material. Having played saxophone and trumpet for many years David already had a solid musical platform when he started to play the harmonica at age fourteen. By age sixteen he was already playing blues jam sessions and harmonica shows in the California Bay Area. By age eighteen he was studying music theory in college and started teaching harmonica at local music institutes. By age twenty he released his first book *Building Harmonica Technique* with Mel Bay Publications. While working to complete his degree in music he had the opportunity to manage a local music store that helped spur the beginning of the Harmonica Masterclass Workshop. David now runs the Harmonica Masterclass Company full time, bringing lesson books, CDs, videos, private instruction, and workshops to players all around the world. His last large workshop had twenty-six states and eight countries represented in attendance. Along with writing for multiple eZines, David also writes a monthly column for Blues Revue Magazine called "Right On The Number." David is also the owner of School of the Blues in San Jose, California. David accepts fly-in lessons on a regular basis. Visit www.schooloftheblues.com for information regarding private lessons.

David has worked and played with Charlie Musselwhite, Mark Hummel, Lee Oskar, Rod Piazza, James Harman, James Cotton, Gary Smith, Andy Just, Mark Ford, Billy Boy Arnold, Rick Estrin, Paul deLay, Jerry Portnoy, Gary Primich, Howard Levy, Magic Dick, Tom Ball, Sonny Jr., Annie Raines, Paul Oscher, Phil Wiggins, Brendan Power, Sam Myers, Snooky Pryor, Rob Paparozzi, Dennis Gruenling, Andy Santana, Carlos del Junco, Mitch Kashmar, Joe Filisko, Steve Freund, Jr. Watson, and John Garcia. He now fronts his own band featuring John Garcia on guitar and vocals.

EXCELLENCE IN MUSIC

MEL BAY®

Since 1947